JAPANESE DETAIL
FASHION

Sadao Hibi

CHRONICLE BOOKS ■ **SAN FRANCISCO**

First published in the United States 1989 by Chronicle Books.
Copyright © 1987 by Sadao Hibi.
First published in Japan by Graphic-sha Publishing Co., Ltd.
All rights reserved. No part of this book may be reproduced in
any form without written permission from Chronicle Books.
Printed in Japan.

Library of Congress Cataloging-in-Publication Data

Hibi, Sadao, 1947–
        [Nihon no dentō iro to katachi, i. English]
        Japanese detail, fashion / Sadao Hibi.
             p.   cm.
        Translation of: Nihon no dentō iro to katachi, i.
        ISBN 0-87701-587-2
        1. Kimonos—Themes, motives.   2. Textile fabrics—
Japan—Themes, motives.   3. Fukusa—Themes, motives.
4. Toilet paraphernalia—Japan—Themes, motives.
5. Smoking paraphernalia—Japan—Themes, motives.
6. Fashion—Japan—Themes, motives.   I. Title.
NK8984.A1H5413   1989
390'.0952—dc19   88-30290
                                                                                   CIP

Distributed in Canada by Raincoast Books,
112 East Third Avenue, Vancouver, B.C. V5T 1C8
Cover design by Karen Pike
10   9   8   7   6   5   4   3   2   1

Chronicle Books
275 Fifth Street
San Francisco, California 94103

CONTENTS

Nostalgia for Color and Form: The Kimono

Ayako Jindai

I can still vividly recall the childhood thrill of sliding my arm into the sleeve of a traditional Japanese kimono for the very first time. It was the morning of the Seven-Five-Three Festival. Later that autumn day, after we returned from offering our prayers at the shrine, Mother was bewildered by my stubborn refusal to shed the brilliantly colored garment.

For many other young women, the kimono is first worn in spring on Adult's Day, when Japanese celebrate their twentieth year and bid farewell to youth. This occasion calls for an elegant, long-sleeved *furisode*, a special gift from one's parents that holds enormous sentimental value. Glancing in the mirror, the *furisode*-clad young woman views herself in a new and splendid guise that she finds deeply touching.

Whatever the event, a woman's eyes always sparkle and her spirits rise upon seeing herself in her first kimono. With each tightening of the braids at the waist, the straight-cut, flat-surfaced dress follows the contour of the body to define a three-dimensional figure of form and grace. To watch the kimono assume its final fit in the mirror is to be filled with the pleasure of being "kimono dressed," an experience that uniquely links a young woman to countless Japanese generations before her.

"Waistcloth tightened is waistline enlivened," is a playful haiku of the Edo period that is at once a keen observation and a naughty commentary on Japanese fashion. Contradictory though it may sound, the tightening of the underbraid and undersash in the Japanese dressing ritual does not deprive the wearer of freedom, but rather enlivens her poise. This heightened confidence is especially conspicuous when a kimono-clad woman is in a crowd of her Western-dressed counterparts.

Ango Sakaguchi, an author-gallant known for his escapades in the play quarters of Kyoto's Gion, once expressed surprise at how dance performers, who go practically unnoticed at teahouses, stand out over other women at Western dance halls. In his highly unconventional thesis, "Personal Views on Japanese Culture," Sakaguchi recalls being quite overcome by the sheer attractive magnetism of the kimono and dangling sash of a Japanese dancing girl. "Though the ancient temples of Kyoto and Nara may burn to the ground," he wrote of this moment, "Japan's tradition quivers not a bit."

The evolution of the kimono reaches far back into Japan's history. By the height of the Heian period, more than a thousand years ago, a formal aesthetic for the garment had already taken shape and begun to play a role in literature. In the Tamakazura chapter in *Tale of Genji*, for instance, Prince Genji, in the presence of Lady Jurasaki, selects kimonos as New Year's gifts for many ladies. Each lady's personality is fully considered by her royal patron, and then color and design are carefully chosen to suit her.

The most representative piece in the Heian wardrobe is the *junihitoe* ceremonial robe. The beauty of both the dress and its ornaments draws on the prominence of *kasaneirome*, a bounty of color arrangements that govern the kimono's neckline, sleeves, and hem. The *kasaneirome* colors reflect the flowers of the four seasons that are the kimono's themes: willow, cherry, Japanese rose, apricot, wisteria, iris, pink Japanese sunflower, bush clover, aster, heliotrope, bellflower, gentian, chrysanthemum, saxifrage. The effect suggests the resplendence of grand gardens.

The prolific and astute use of colors cultivated by Heian court nobles has, with some changes, continued to the present. In the past, this refinement was not limited to the nobility, however. The samurai, or warrior class, also showed a strong partiality for brilliant colors, as revealed in *Tales of Heike*, one of the first Japanese war annals. The armor of warlords is described in detail, as in this elaborate portrait of famous General Sanemori Saito moments before his death:

A grass-green suit of braided armor covers his brocaded court dress of red, and the straps of his hoe-crested helmet are firmly tightened. Sporting golden swords at his side and grasping a rattan-striped bow in his hands with twenty-notched arrows hanging on his back, he sits firmly in a gold-trimmed saddle on his dapple-gray steed.

Warriors like Saito held strongly to the tradition of dressing in fine clothes before departing for a battleground, even though fully resigned to death. This practice is exquisitely illustrated in a number of antique scrolls and screens depicting Heian-era military battles.

The flowers connected with the *kasaneirome* color scheme illustrate the importance that the Japanese have always placed on nurturing a strong communion with nature. In ancient literature, one finds plants used for making textile dyes, such as madder (red) and cromwell (purple), are frequently mentioned to convey feeling:

My beloved lord [Prince Oama] strolls among the lush cromwells of Bamo, beckoning me with his sleeves aflutter. I dread the gardener's eyes.

My love for you is greater than the pain of scandal. For how could I love another's wife as beautiful as these cromwells if indeed she disliked me.

This famous pair of answering love poems, which appears in the first chapter of the *Manyōshū*, was written during a hunting expedition Prince Oama took in the company of Emperor Tenchi in Gamono, in the Omi district. At the time, cromwells were cultivated for producing dyes at the imperial estate of Shimeno in Gamono. The fragrant fields of cromwells add a certain brilliance to these charming verses praising love's noble passions.

In addition to adopting colors and motifs directly from nature, the Japanese have also created a vast treasure of designs abstracted from natural elements. In searching for themes in nature, they cast their attention not only on flowers and birds or such familiar landscape subjects as the bright moon and the cool breeze, but even on a host of insects. The *mushizukushi monkataginu*, a costume worn in Kyogen farces by the Shigeyamas of the Daizo School of Noh, is a classic example. A huge praying mantis with a large snail crawling beneath it is fully displayed on the back of the Noh costume. Spiders, wasps, grasshoppers, and other bugs also appear in humorous detail. The depictions reveal the wit-filled spirit of a people deeply attached to the soil, the presence of laughter in everyday rural life.

The arts of textile coloring and weaving are equally complex in their intent, as they subtly condense the life of the environment. This is the world of natural dyes, of deriving tints and shades from flowers, fruits, leaves, barks, and roots of plants. In *One Color, One Lifetime*, Fukumi Shimura, a weaver and dyer for nearly thirty years, describes her enlightenment:

> Some time back it occurred to me that the dyes derived from plants were not significant only for the colors they yielded. For I had finally come to realize that the very lives of plants were embraced in the dyes that the plants offered to us.

Such sentiments could only be those of a person who maintains an especially reverential regard for nature, and who truly believes that natural colors are not merely for the taking. They are nature's precious gifts.

This may explain why natural indigo is undergoing a quiet boom in an age where the gap between man and nature continues to widen. New patterns utilizing the color are turning up everywhere, even on luncheon mats and napkins. Indigo is an extremely complicated and esoteric dyeing material; the smallest indigo-colored object is a testament to nature's mysteries. Thus, the proliferation of such objects affirms nature's continuing power to move us. They remind us that the door closing man in can be opened, if only we will maintain a dialogue with the natural world beyond its threshold.

Patterns of the Kimono

Masafumi Sugai

Last summer, I attended an exhibition on Thailand at the Tokyo National Museum. I had hoped to find dyed and woven materials of minority groups, but none were included. Instead I saw an extraordinary sculpture of a young girl, which immediately filled me with supreme bliss. She had long, fragile hands and a youthful smile reminiscent of the Maitreya Bodhisattva of the Koryuji and Chiguji temples.

There were also photographs of Buddhist temples that movingly captured the structures' solemnity, and paintings and ornamental crafts that to my eye closely resembled the imperial properties stored in Nara's Shosoin repository. One piece in particular, a stone carving of what appeared to be a holy linden tree with a man, sheep, and lions playing at its base, recalled the permanent exhibits at both Shosoin and Horyugi Temple. The experience again put me in mind of Japan's modern attachment to the West, and its far greater commonality of culture with the countries of Southeast Asia.

The permanent exhibits of the Tokyo National Museum are always a joy to behold. A display of rare attire from the early Edo period was on view there at the same time that I went to see the Thailand show. Included was a splendid court dress that had been passed down through generations to today's princely Takamatsu line. This bloodline, which leads to the imperial throne, was itself established during the early days of Edo. A list of the occasions on which former emperors and princes had worn the costumes was posted.

The exhibit illustrated how the skillfully woven patterns and designs appearing on imperial costumes were strictly regulated according to the wearer's degree of nobility, rank, and the time of the year. Imperial and military designs such as the hollyhock and triple sash appeared repeatedly. Elsewhere, cranes and chrysanthemums were embroidered in very large patterns to express the exceptional lineage of the owner. The *junihitoe* ceremonial robe, an impressive but very heavy, uncomfortable kimono worn by court wives, dramatized another feature of the court kimono tradition: the extremely high cost in time and materials required to weave these elaborate costumes.

A bit exhausted, I proceeded to the gallery downstairs that holds a permanent show of Japanese dyed and woven materials. The room contained works of art that graphically reflected how diverse tastes could be in the past, with examples ranging from fantasy-driven stark geometric designs to realistic landscape paintings.

Among them was a cloudy white wadded-silk garment under a dim light, suggestive of sunlight filtered by a shoji screen. Here was the withered tree of winter transposed onto a silk garment—the world of Ogata Korin and his india-ink paintings of autumn foliage, chrysanthemum, bellflower, bush clover, pampas grass, and other plants printed on a white background.

Reproductions of Korin's paintings appear in many books, but nothing is more enjoyable than coming upon the actual works of the master. With his effortless use of contrasting ink shades and bold and light brush strokes, he perfectly expresses the gray leaves of the bush clover, the lemon-yellow tinge of the chrysanthemum, the green of the bellflower, and the golden ribs of the pampas grass. The foliage of fall is graphically portrayed in grassy fields familiar to all Japanese; Korin's silent painted world even conjures the cries of the ringbell insect as it is carried along in the autumn wind. How appropriate this design must have been for the wife of the Fuyuki clan, one of many lumber merchants in Fukagawa. I tried to imagine her garbed in this exquisite design.

While Korin's best-known paintings and sketches impress us with his talent as an interpreter of flowers and birds, he also had an interest in drawing women. True, in the "Hundred Sketches of Korin," his portraits of characters from Heian tales—full-cheeked faces and up-turned chins—are rather mundane. Yet his "Sketches of Women" show a model in a standing pose that captures the animated atmosphere of the age eloquently, and probably lives up to his ideal of female beauty.

There is also a sketch of a woman extending her left hand from her kimono sleeve and resting it on her hip while her right hand, slipped into a wrap below the front sash, lifts the gusset. Dresses in this age were typified by long hems, and sketches of beautiful women invariably showed their right hands turning the hems upward slightly. Korin's departure from this standard form is a bold statement. Wadded-silk garments of the day were without patterns, and for this reason the movement of the left hand determined the flow of the sleeve, which in turn enabled one to assess the shape and maturity of the body.

What sort of kimono design would suit Korin's lady? The question is not superfluous. An anecdote in the *Comparison of Kimonos* tells of an older gentleman arranging a battle dress of pure white on a background of black *habutae* silk for the wife of his friend, Nakamura Kuranosuke, and winning the admiration of peers for his brilliance.

As for prevailing fashions in the third year of Kambun, as suggested by an order book of a dry-goods dealer, the outstanding feature of design was its extremely large size; the robe flowed straight from the shoulders to the hem. The majority of the era's designs also had a large unbroken area, reaching from under the arm to the floor, on which a pattern was drawn. In a survey of records for more than 500 kimono designs, about 350 employed white or blackish red as the background color.

Korin, who was born into a family engaged in dyeing and weaving, is known to have mastered the technique of producing dyed, woven materials. His pine patterns on a white wadded-silk garment in "Introduction of Sensual Patterns," printed in the twelfth year of Genroku, are often cited as examples of his influence in this area. The garment in question was commissioned by a dilettante of the period who cultivated talented clothiers, painters, and other artists; such patrons belonged to the wealthy merchant class then striving to outshine the warrior class. Eventually a stage was reached in which the aim was to display the latest design on a wadded-silk garment mounted on a clothes rack, much as one would display a silk screen. No one is certain of the authenticity of works identified as Korin's, however, except for those owned by the Fuyuki family. In fact, Korin probably entertained much more interest in painting, pottery, and lacquerwork than he did in kimono design.

Painter Hishikawa Motonobu, a genius who preceded Korin by about two centuries, was born the son of a famous artist of Yasuda, Taira, in Awa Province. Motonobu inherited from his father the skills of the artisan and the strong spirit of the craftsman. As a boy, he was instructed in the arts of the tea ceremony, flower arrangement, and singing and dancing, and improved himself further through the study of books, pictorial arts, and calligraphy. At the age of thirty, he went to Edo to work. He found the city vibrant, filled with a dynamism directed toward recovering from the Great Fire of Meireki. It was an age when picture books were being published and print culture was becoming popular among the masses.

For his "Hundred Women of Japan," Motonobu surveyed women's many roles, while his "Sketches of Occupations in Japan" looked at society's traditional artisans and craftsmen. He produced a number of pillow pictures, all of which were quite cheerful; none bordered on the obscene, as was the case with those censored by a future generation. It is estimated that Motonobu created over 130 pictures and picture books, a number that almost certainly overwhelmed the artist attendants of the shogunate.

In Motonobu's vivid portrayals of the manners and customs of the Yoshiwara streets, the people's garments display forms and designs indicating occupation and social status. While fads and fashions are often short-lived, the publishing of these illustrations hastened the spread of trends to the outlying districts. The patterns and designs printed over a 150-year period, during the sixth and seventh years of Kambun until the Bunsei reign of the shogunate, brightened women's lives with a steady supply of new garments.

The patterns believed to be the work of Motonobu are the *shinban kosode hinagata*, *onhinagata manyōshū*, and *shinban tofu onhinagata*. Carefully studied, a Motonobu pattern is quite interesting. As I glanced through the "Hundred Women of Japan," I noticed that many large single patterns—the cherry blossom, chrysanthemum, cloud, whirlpool, Chinese flower, fan, autumn leaf, paulownia, wood sorrel, seven treasures, *rokuyosei*, *enbishi*, *jakago*, and others—are spread evenly throughout the pages. While the patterns are not perfectly clear because the backs of many of the garments are obscured, one can see that they are completely different from the flowing designs of the Kambun wadded-silk garments that span the shoulder-to-hem area.

Initially it appears as if these singular patterns did not differ from the concepts of court and military design, but I tend to believe that a difference did exist, since designs depended upon the dyes that were applied. Moreover, creating large designs and positioning them evenly into spaces could have been done easily and cheaply, and the widespread publishing of picture books had made the designs part of popular culture.

Motonobu may have preferred these designs. His "Beauty Glancing Back" (Tokyo National Museum collection) sports small flowers on a red background neatly arranged in the manner of court and military designs, with large cherry blossom and chrysanthemum designs well positioned on the back, hem, and both sleeves. Appropriate for young girls from families of high social standing, these designs were as time-consuming and expensive to produce as court and military patterns. Yet they were also quite prevalent, and their use reflects the artist's own orthodox life-style and rejection of the unconventional.

In this respect, the appearances of Korin and Motonobu on the historical stage might have more appropriately occurred in reverse. The extensive distribution of patterns and picture books meant that aspects of high culture in old Kyoto and Osaka were widely adopted in Edo. Had Korin been alive, he would have thoroughly disapproved. This is not to say that Korin's work lost its relevance, however. His designs, characterized by round shapes, emphasized a sense of fullness set off by toned-down contours. While his plum designs appear most frequently, he nevertheless continued to produce designs depicting the petals of flowers and the veins of leaves in abbreviated forms, highly appreciated then and by generations to follow.

Before Motonobu and Korin made their unique marks on the world of design, the production of kimonos depended primarily upon the ingenuity of craftsmen, much as it does today. But the contributions of these two giants to the beauty of the kimono spoke to an underlying aesthetic, rather than to quality of production, and therefore merit special attention.

Moreover, they dramatize the extent to which no full study of the kimono can be conducted without including the lives of the artists who shaped its evolution.

Selected Bibliography: *Genroku Jidai*, by Oishi Shinsauro (Iwanami Shinsho, 1970). *Ogata Korin*, by Kono Motoaki (From *Nihon Bijutsu Kaiga Zenshu*, Shueisha, 1980). *Hishikawa Motonobu Genroku Onna-E Zukushi*, by Omori Takayuki (1979), *Nihon no Kimono*, by Tatsumura Ken (Chuko Shinsha, 1966). *Korin*, by Chizawa Teiji (Shibundo, 1970).

1. Hawk and wooden screen pattern (*taka, tsuitate*)

2 . Washing *yuzen* cloth

4 . Rice-planting festival

5. Antique toilet set

6. Empress doll

FIGURES AND PATTERNS

文様

The rich natural world gave rise to various figures and patterns used on clothing: clouds moving across the sky, and the flowers, birds, and animals of the four seasons. The designs and colors provide material for a visual feast.

8 . Lightning pattern (*kaminari*)

9 . Swords-in-wood-sorrel pattern on tortoiseshell pattern (*kenkatabami, kikko*)

18

10. Tortoiseshell pattern on *tachiwaki* pattern

11. Flowers-in-overlapping-circles pattern (*hana shippō tsunagi*)

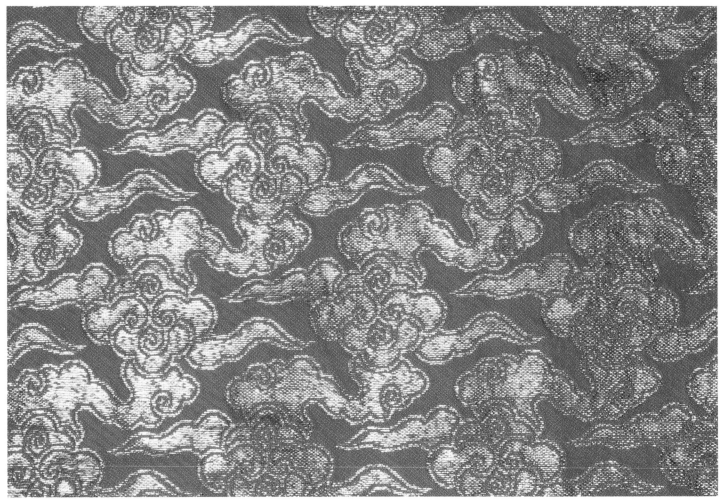

12. Cloud pattern (*kumo*)

13. Flowing water pattern (*ryūsui*)

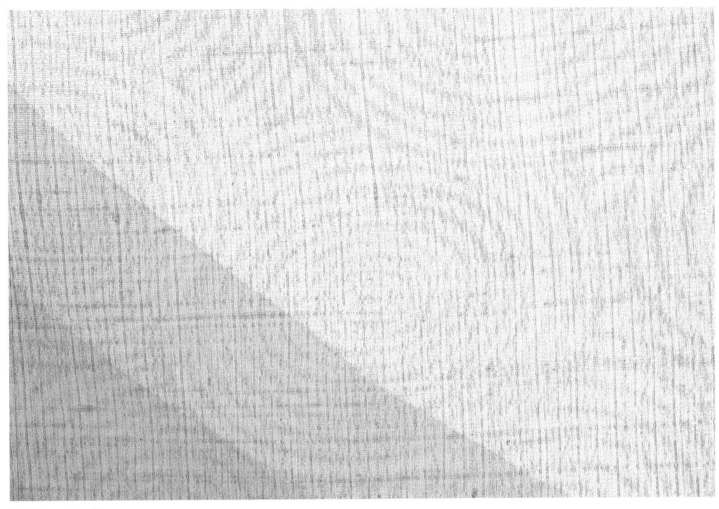

14. Swirl pattern (*uzumaki*)

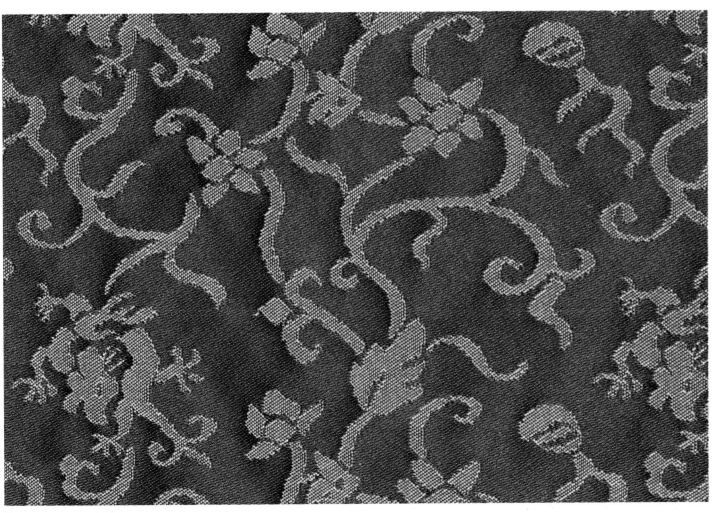

15. Arabesque pattern (*karakusa*)

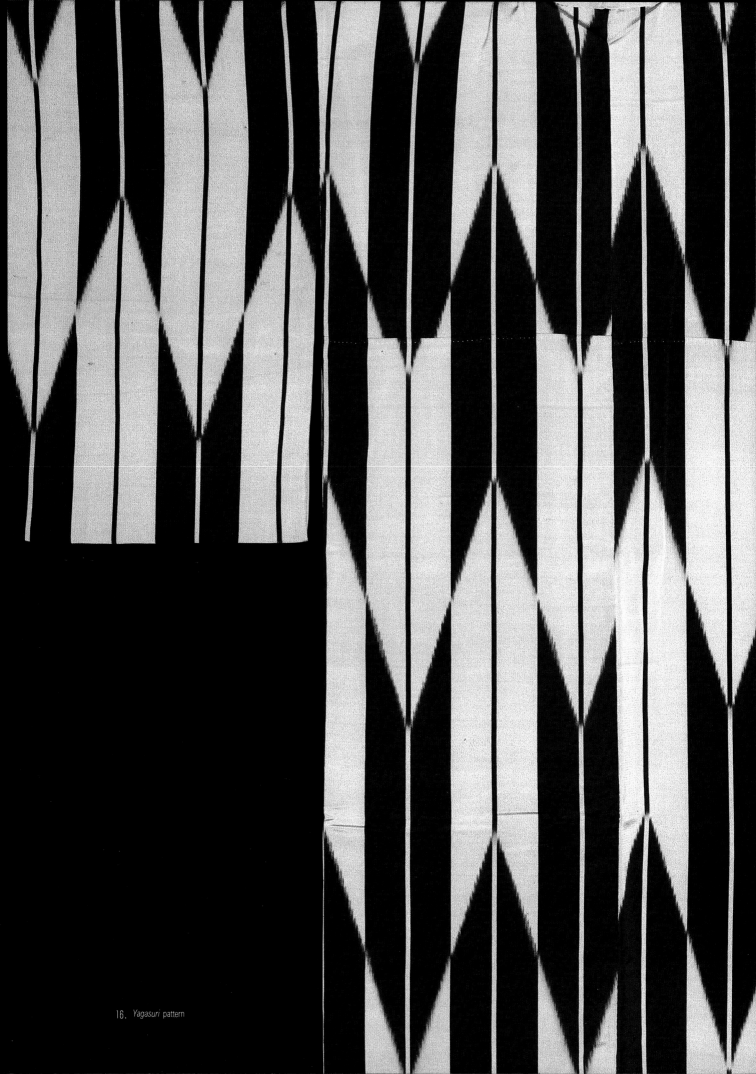

16. *Yagasuri* pattern

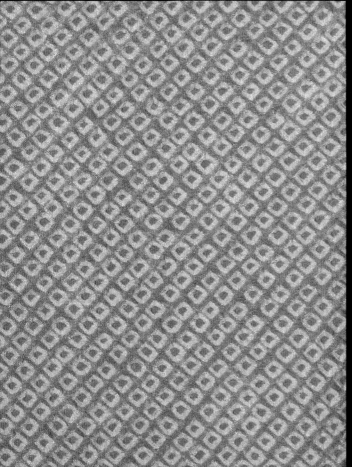

17. A dappled tie-dye pattern (*sôshibori*)

18. Overlapping waves pattern (*seigaiha*) (Tokyo National Museum)

19. "Connected nine-stones" pattern (*tsunagi kokonotsu ishi*)

20. Fish scale pattern (*uroko*)

21. Cypress fence pattern (*higaki*)

22. Scattered maple-leaf pattern on pine-bark pattern (*momiji, chirashi, matsukawa-bishi*)

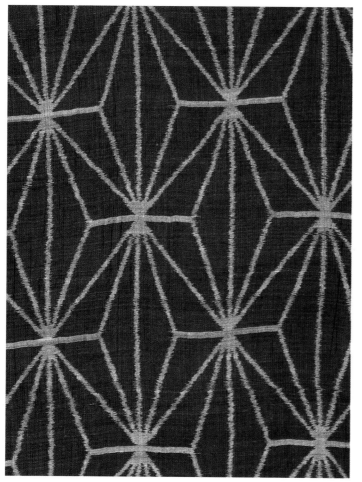

23. Joined hemp leaf pattern (*asa-no-ha tsunagi*)

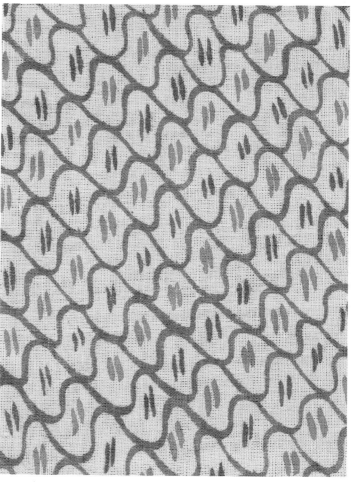

24. Net pattern (*ami-no-me*)

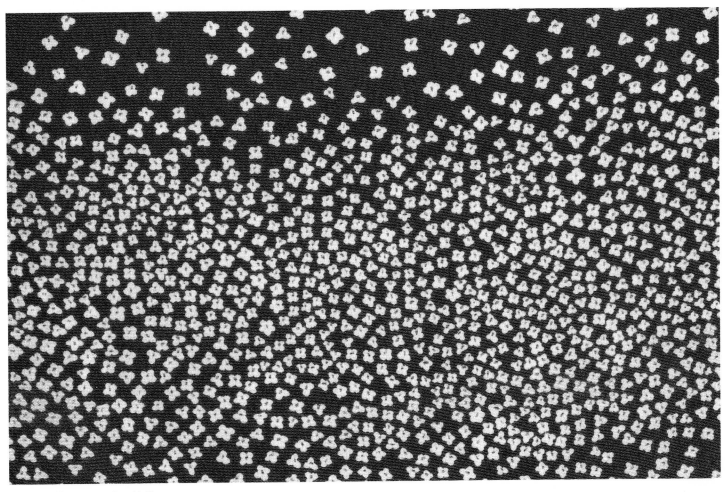

25. Blizzard of flowers pattern (*hana fubuki*)

26. Fine sharkskin pattern (*samehada*)

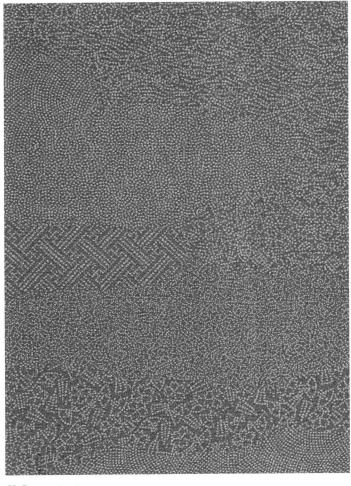

27. Fine *yosegata* pattern

28. Phoenix and paulownias on an arabesque pattern (*karakusa*)

29. Dragons on a cloud pattern.

30. Fish pattern (*sakana*)

31. Flying cranes pattern (*hikaku*)

32. Cranes pattern

33. Folded-cranes pattern (*orizuru*)

28

34. Butterfly pattern (*chō*)

35. Butterfly pattern

36. Butterfly pattern

37. Chrysanthemum pattern (*kikka*)

38. Pine pattern (*matsu*)

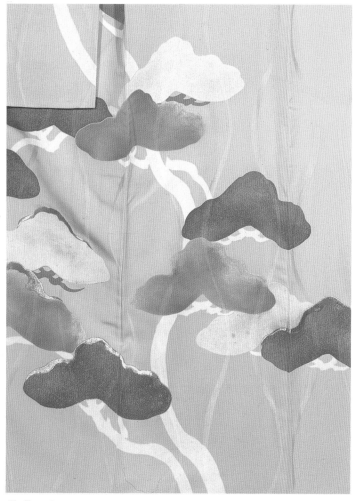

39. Pine pattern

40. Pattern based on a scene of Sumiyoshi Bay

41. Chrysanthemum pattern on a fence pattern (*kikka, kakine*)

42. Chrysanthemum-and-autumn-flowers pattern (*kikku akikusa*)

43. Chrysanthemum pattern (*kikka*)

44. Maple pattern (*kaede*)

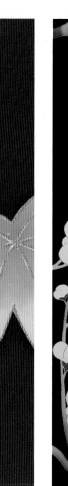

45. Red-and-white plum pattern (*kōhakubai*)

46. Maple leaf pattern (*momiji*)

47. Bamboo and red-and-white plum pattern (*take, kōhakubai*)

48. Cherry blossom and violet pattern (*sakura, sumire*)

49. White bush clover pattern (*shirohagi*)

50. Camellia pattern (*tsubaki*)

51. Hydrangea pattern (*ajisai*)

52. Bellflower pattern (*kikyō*)

53. Flowers-in-diamonds pattern (*hanabishi*)

54. Orchid pattern (*ran*)

55. Pampas grass and chrysanthemum-butterfly pattern (*susuki, kiku, chō*)

56. Flowing water and grass-and-flower pattern (*ryūsui, kusabana*)

57. Flowing water and grass-and-flower pattern

58. Scenic landscape pattern (*fūkei*)

59. Scenic landscape pattern

60. Plaid pattern (*kōshi-jima*)

. Striped pattern (*shima*)

62. Striped pattern

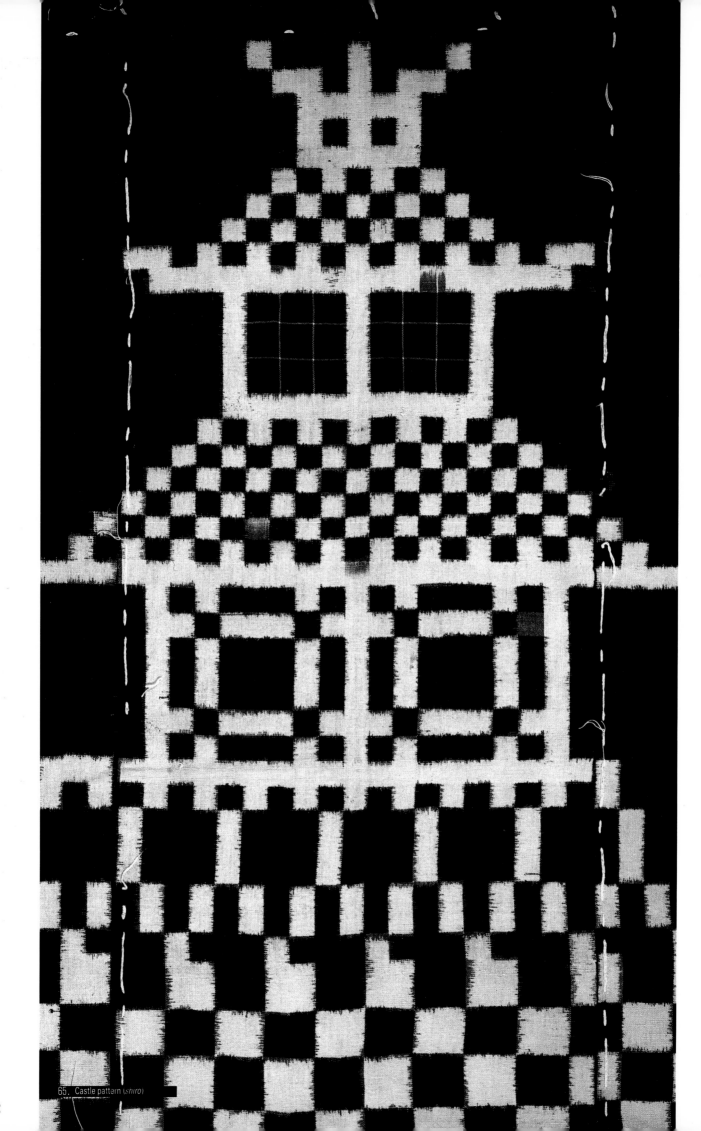

65. Castle pattern (*shiro*)

67. Carp-and-hermit and checked pattern (*koisennin, ichimatsu*)

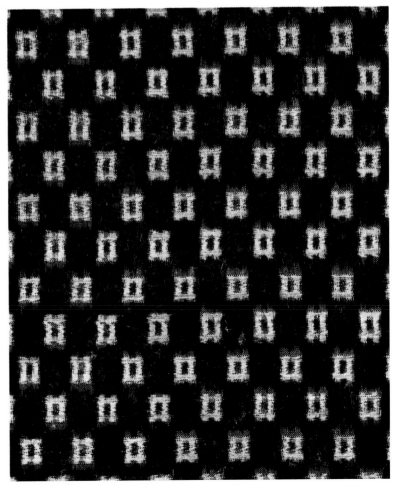

66. Steamboat and geometric pattern (*kisen, kikagaku*)

68. Projecting parallels pattern (*igeta*)

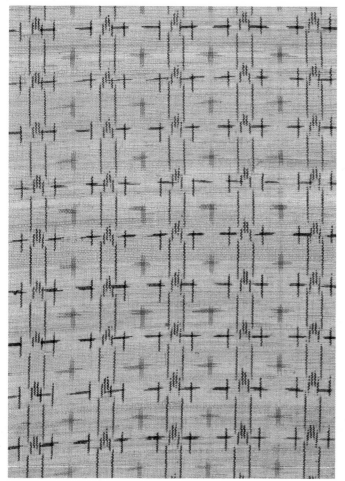

69. Splashed pattern (*kasuri*)

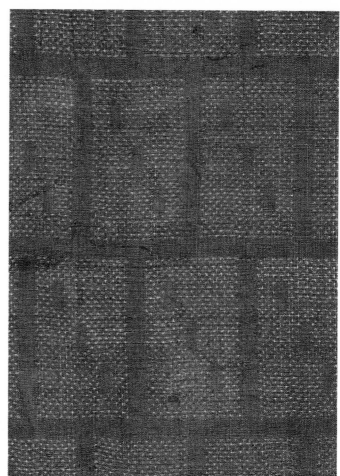

70. Splashed pattern

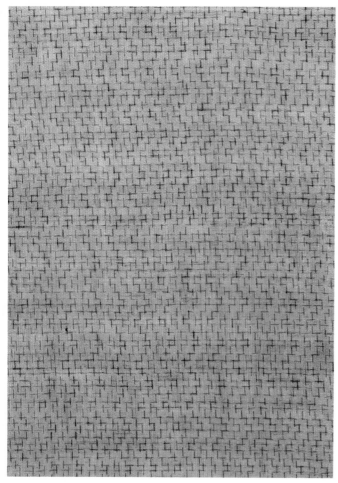

71. Splashed pattern

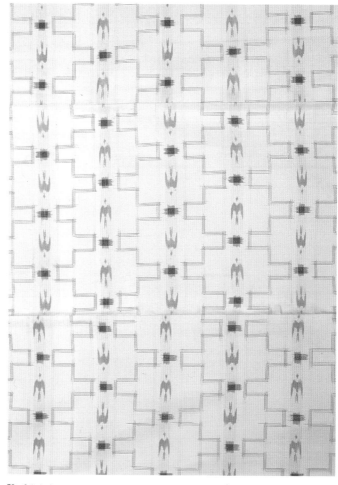

72. Splashed pattern

CLOTHING

衣裳

Clothing carries with it a flow of history and culture: the numerous overlapping kimonos called "the twelve robes," worn by court ladies; the short-sleeved kimono of *Tsujigahana*.

73. "Great poet" pattern (*kasen*)

74. Happi coat with chrysanthemum, peony, and arabesque pattern in gold brocade
on iron-blue cloth

75. *Sobatsugi* with various patterns on yellow cloth

76: *Kariginu* with paulownia pattern in gold brocade on a dark blue field

77. *Atsuita*; flower-in-tortoiseshell and wisteria pattern on a green field (Tokyo National Museum)

78. Noh costume: a *karaori* with a design of butterflies and chrysanthemums on a red and white field

79. Long-sleeved kimono (*furisode*) with cherry blossom and pheasant pattern on grayish blue cotton

80. Short-sleeved *kimono* with *yagasuri* and cherry blossom pattern

81. *Kamishimo* with three-leafed hollyhock pattern

Although the *obi* is, of course, worn with a kimono, it is a work of art in its own right. The beauty of an *obi* is completed when it is tied with an undersash and fine braid.

82. *Obi* with cherry blossom and raft pattern on figured satin

83. Double-layered *obi* (*fukuro-obi*) with *koto* and chrysanthemum pattern

84. Double-layered *obi* with folding fan pattern

85. Double-layered *obi* with paulownia and chrysanthemum pattern

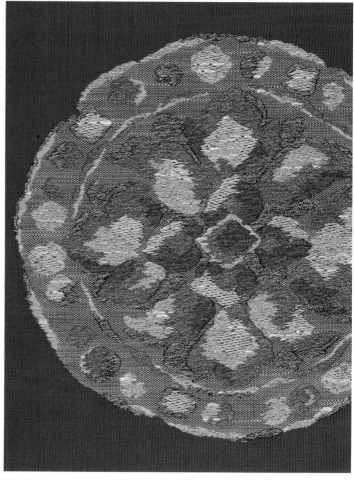

86. *Obi* with *karahana* ("Chinese flower") pattern

87. *Obi* with *kicchō* (lucky omen) pattern

88. *Obi* with flowing water and chrysanthemum pattern

89. Double-layered *obi* with *karahana* pattern

90. *Obi* with autumn flower pattern

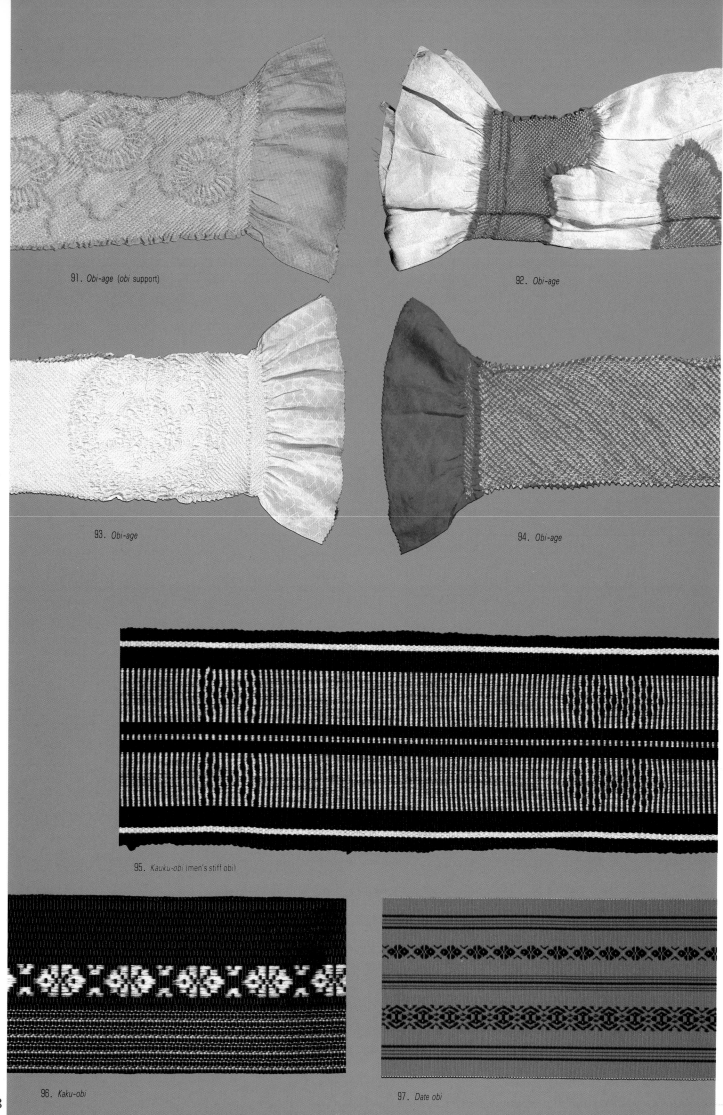

91. *Obi-age* (obi support)

92. *Obi-age*

93. *Obi-age*

94. *Obi-age*

95. *Kaku-obi* (men's stiff obi)

96. *Kaku-obi*

97. *Date obi*

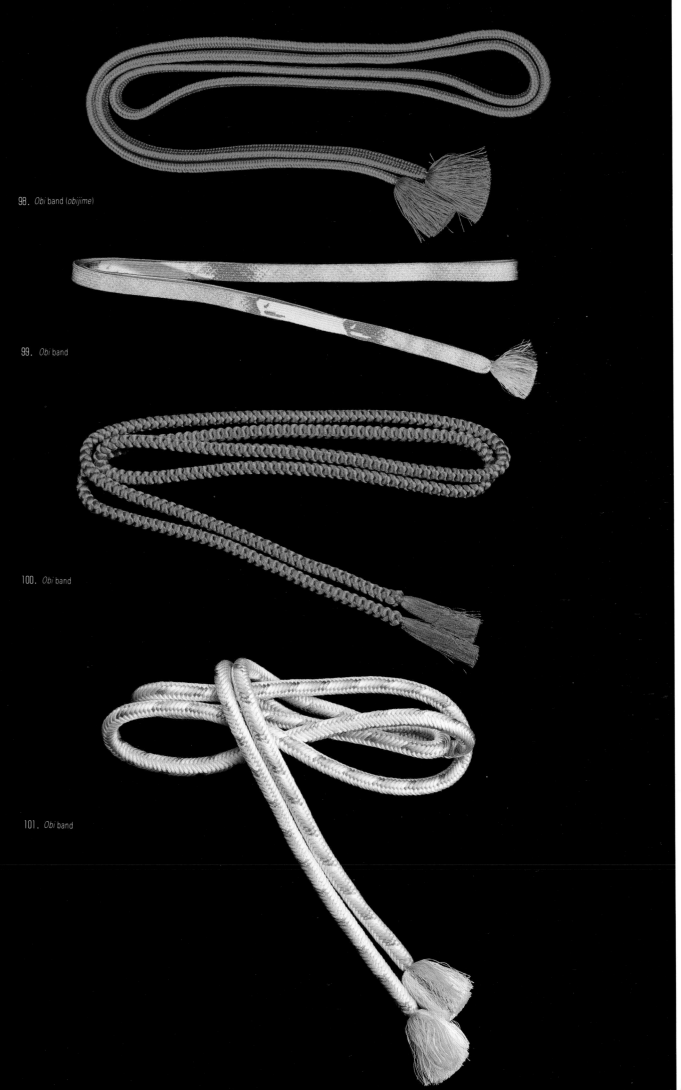

98. *Obi* band (*obijime*)

99. *Obi* band

100. *Obi* band

101. *Obi* band

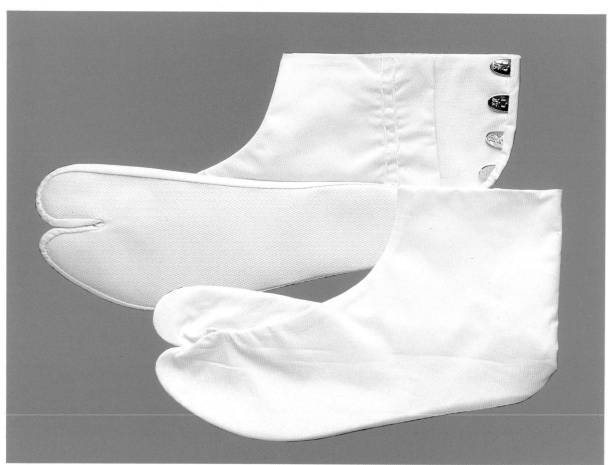

102. White *tabi*

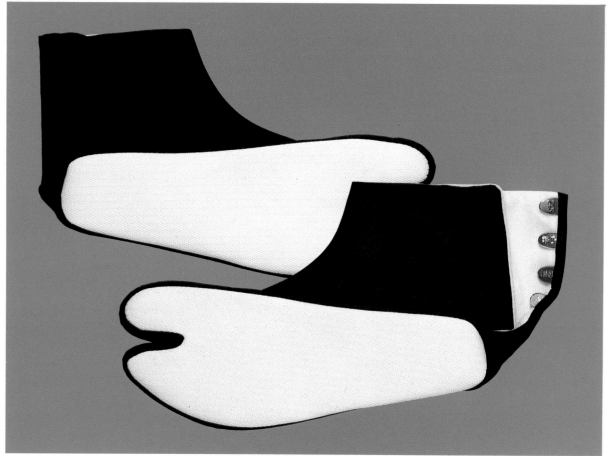

103. Black *tabi*

袱紗

The *fukusa* is a handy square of cloth for wrapping things. Fold it up and it fits neatly in a pocket. Its applications are limited only by the user's imagination.

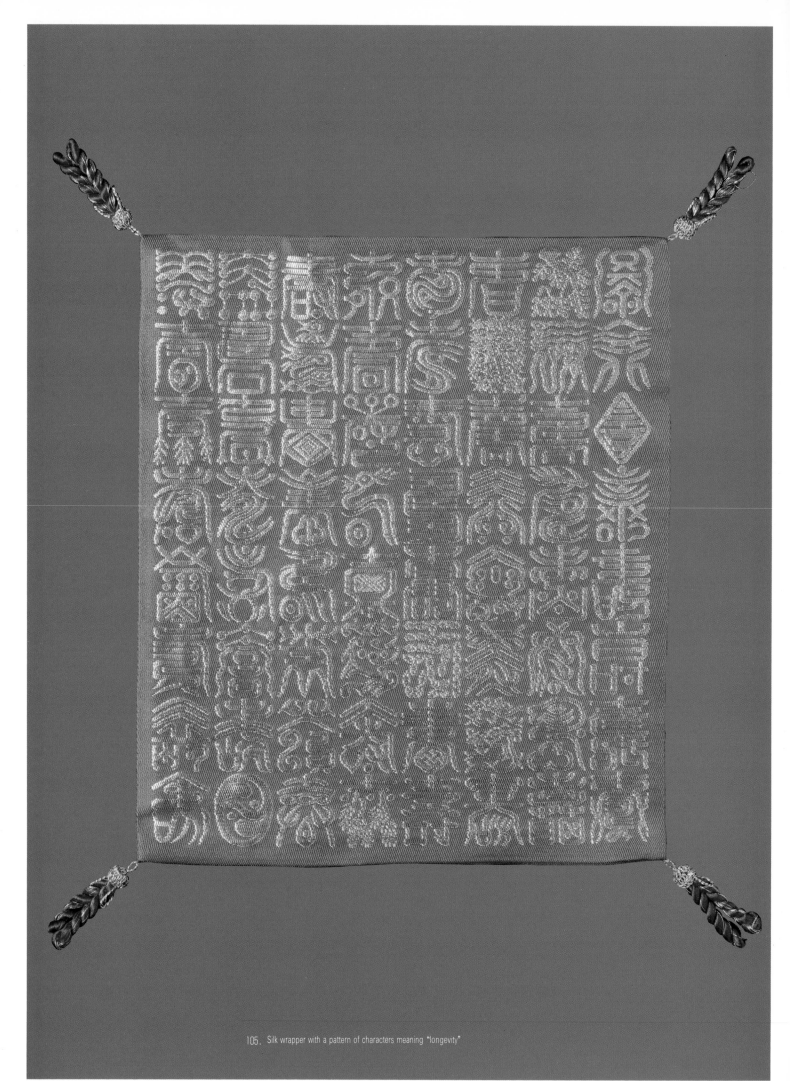

105. Silk wrapper with a pattern of characters meaning "longevity"

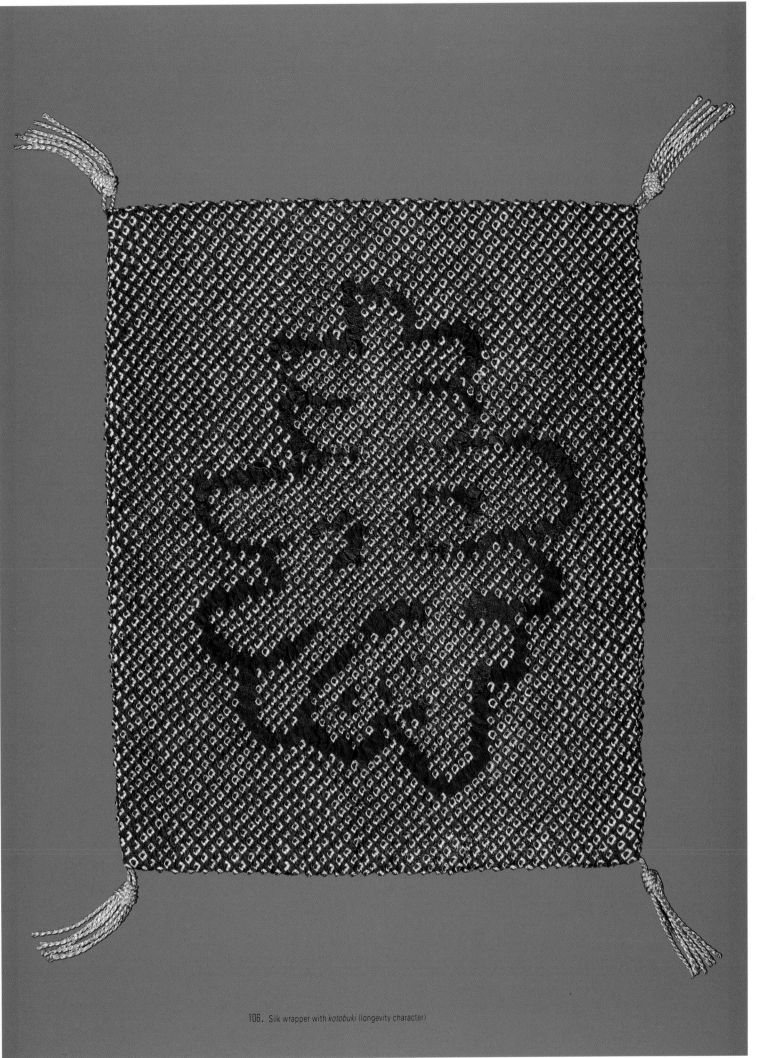

106. Silk wrapper with *kotobuki* (longevity character)

107. Silk wrapper depicting a "treasure boat"

108. Silk wrapper depicting a crayfish

109. Silk wrapper depicting a *manzai* (ancient drama) master

110. Silk wrapper with hemp flower and pattern

111. *Furoshiki* (large wrapping cloth) with crane, turtle, and pine-bamboo-plum pattern

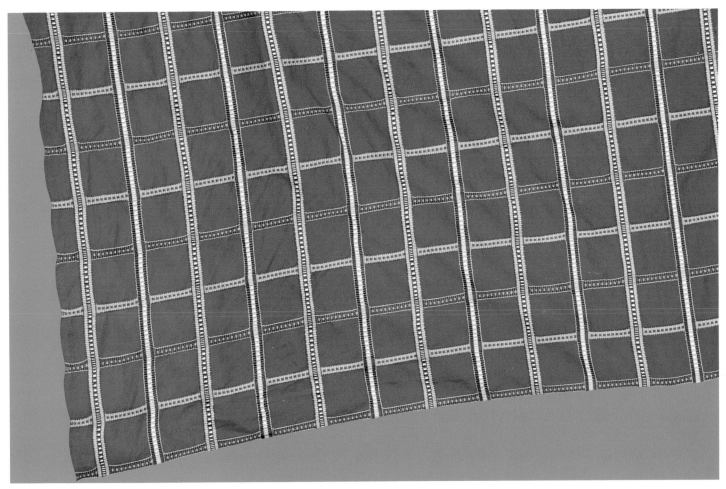

112. *Furoshiki* with *yoshino* lattice pattern

113. *Sukiya* bag

114. *Sukiya* bag

115. Drawstring purse (*kinchaku*)

116. *Inden* (tanned sheepskin) drawstring purse

TOILET ARTICLES

化粧道具

Women of every age have desired to make themselves appealing. A mirror and makeup accessories, carefully chosen by the woman using them, serve to deepen her elegance and refine her beauty.

117. Mirror with pair of cranes and paulownia pattern

118. Mirror with pair of cranes and chrysanthemum pattern

119. Hand mirror with crane and turtle pattern

120. Mirror with "three oak leaves in a circle" crest

121. Mirror with mother-and-child crane pattern

122. Hand mirror with bellflower pattern and
the character *hana* (flower)

123. Box for toilet articles

124. Early toilet articles

125. Jewelry box with lacquerwork, mother-of-pearl, and paulownia and bellflower patterns

71

126. Mirror stand and mirror

COMBS AND HAIRPINS

櫛・簪

Combs can be used for both combing and decorating hair. Long, luxurious black hair has been for centuries the premier distinction of feminine beauty, and women's combs have played an important role in making this so.

127. Comb with maple pattern

128. Tortoiseshell comb with white dove in mother-of-pearl; tortoiseshell ornamental hairpin

129. Comb and ornamental hairpin with water plants and goldfish pattern in mother-of-pearl

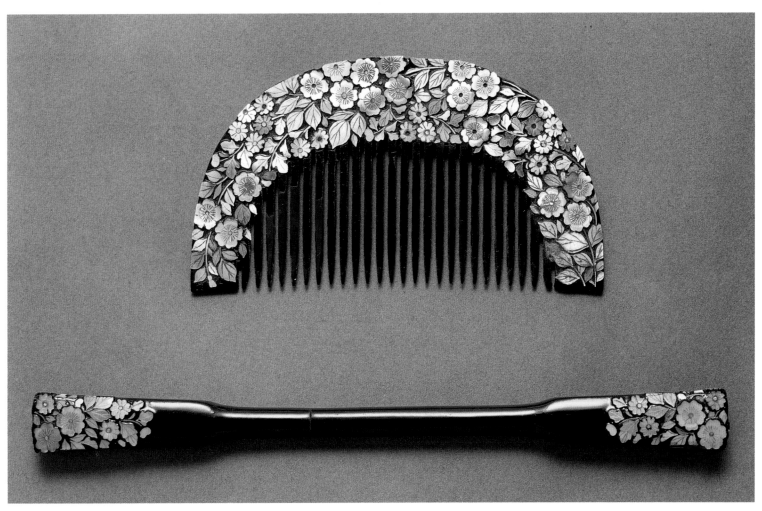

130. Black-lacquered comb and ornamental hairpin with cherry blossom pattern in mother-of-pearl

131. Comb and ornamental hairpin with maple pattern in gold lacquerwork

75

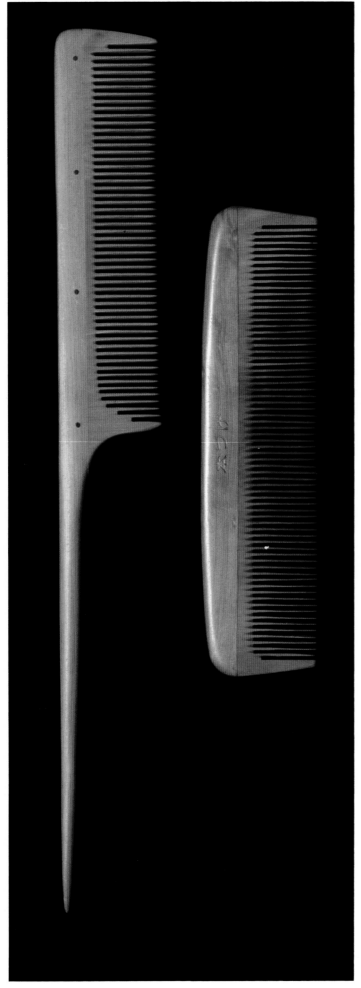

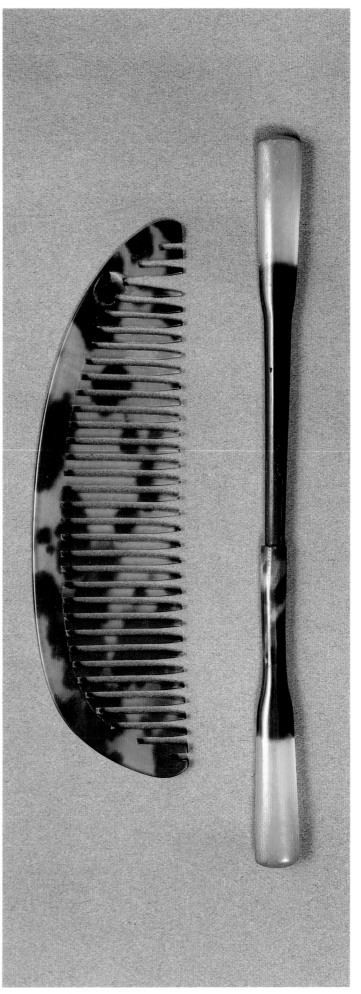

132. Combs

133. Tortoiseshell comb and ornamental hairpin

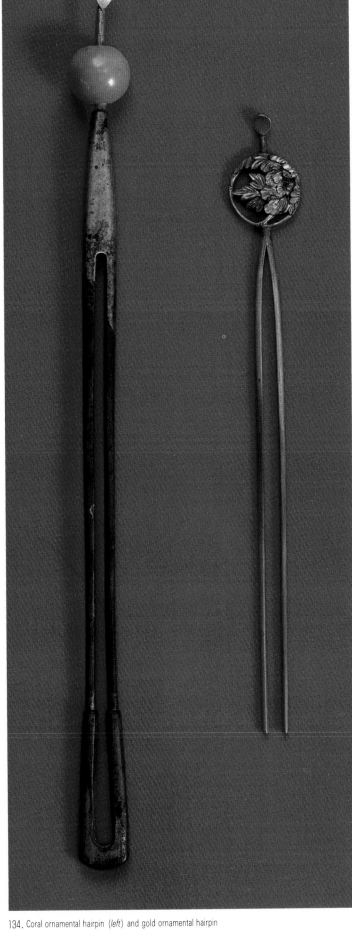

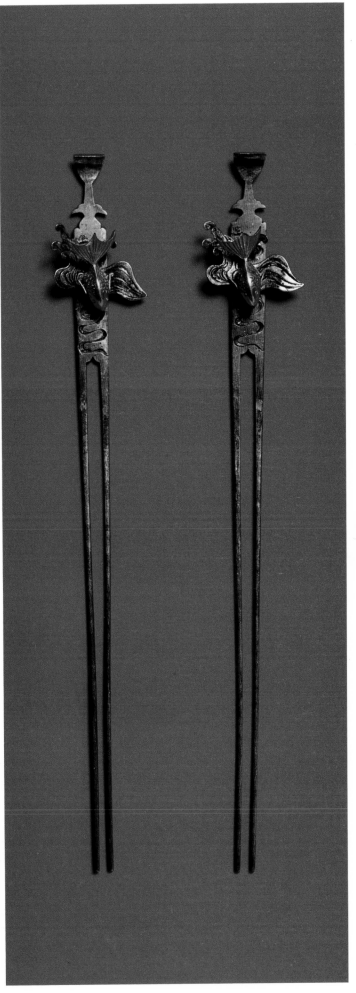

134. Coral ornamental hairpin (*left*) and gold ornamental hairpin

135. Ornamental hairpins decorated with goldfish

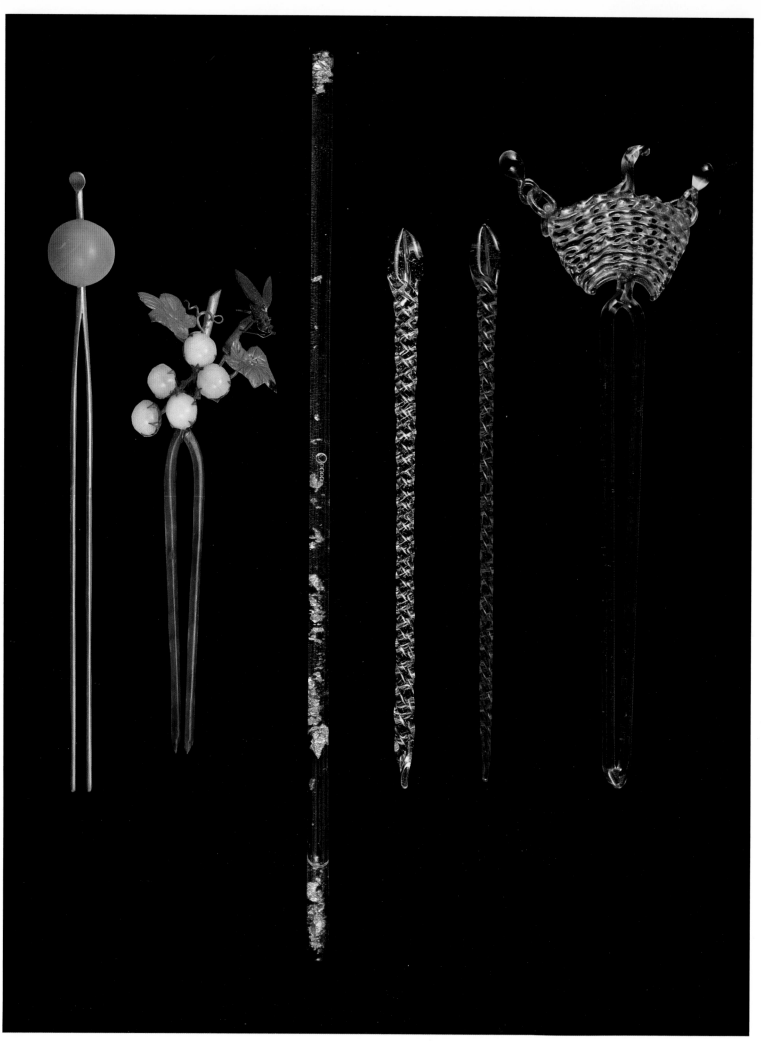

136. Coral ornamental hairpin (*left*) and ornamental hairpin decorated with grapes and a fly

137. Glass ornamental hairpins

菊

桃

梅

葛

138.—141. *Sōtōka* (a kind of hair ornament); chrysanthemums, peach blossoms, plum blossoms, ivy

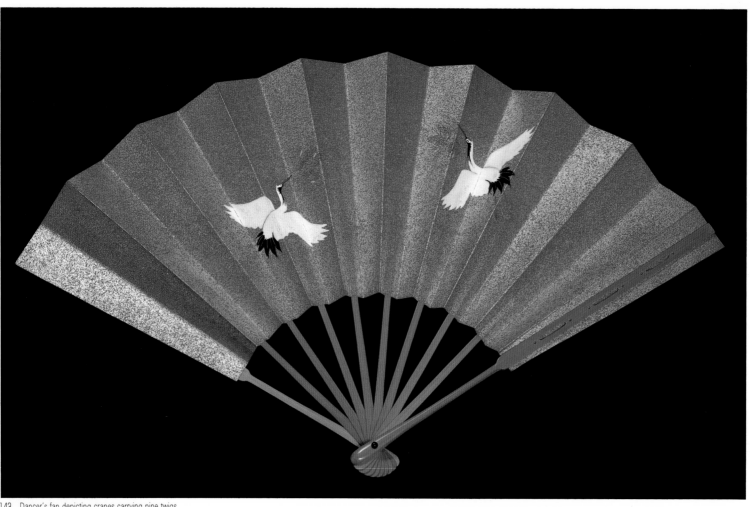

143. Dancer's fan depicting cranes carrying pine twigs

144. Dancer's fan with a pine tree on a gold field

145. Dancer's fan with kite pattern on a gold field

146. Dancer's fan with reed-and-autumn-flowers pattern on a gold field

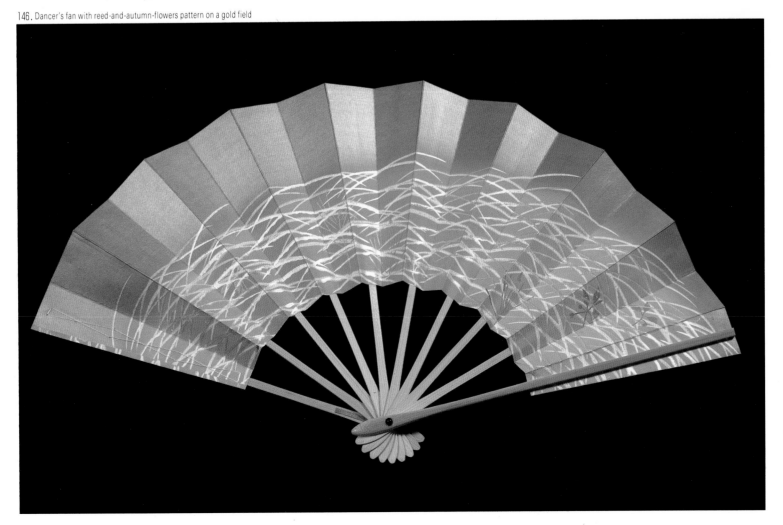

147. Dancer's fan with pine-bamboo-plum pattern on a gold field

148. Dancer's fan with red maple leaf pattern on a silver field

149. Dancer's fan depicting a landscape

150. Dancer's fan depicting the moon

151. Japanese cypress folding fan with red-and-white plum blossom and bamboo pattern

152. Japanese cypress folding fan with pine and red maple leaf pattern

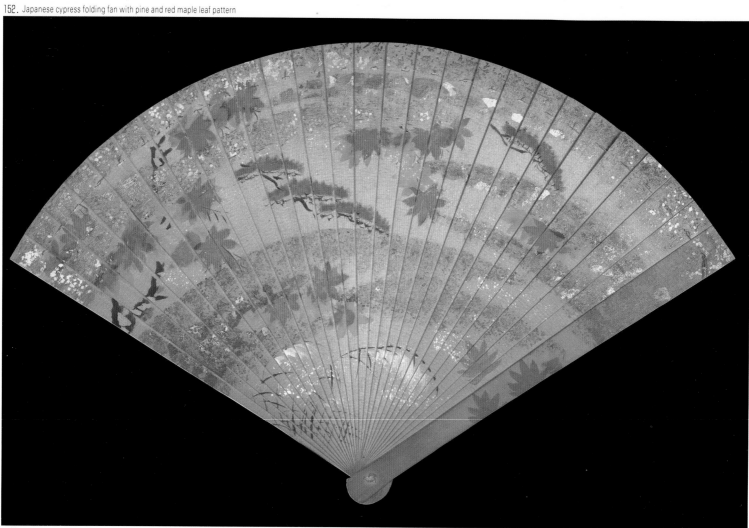

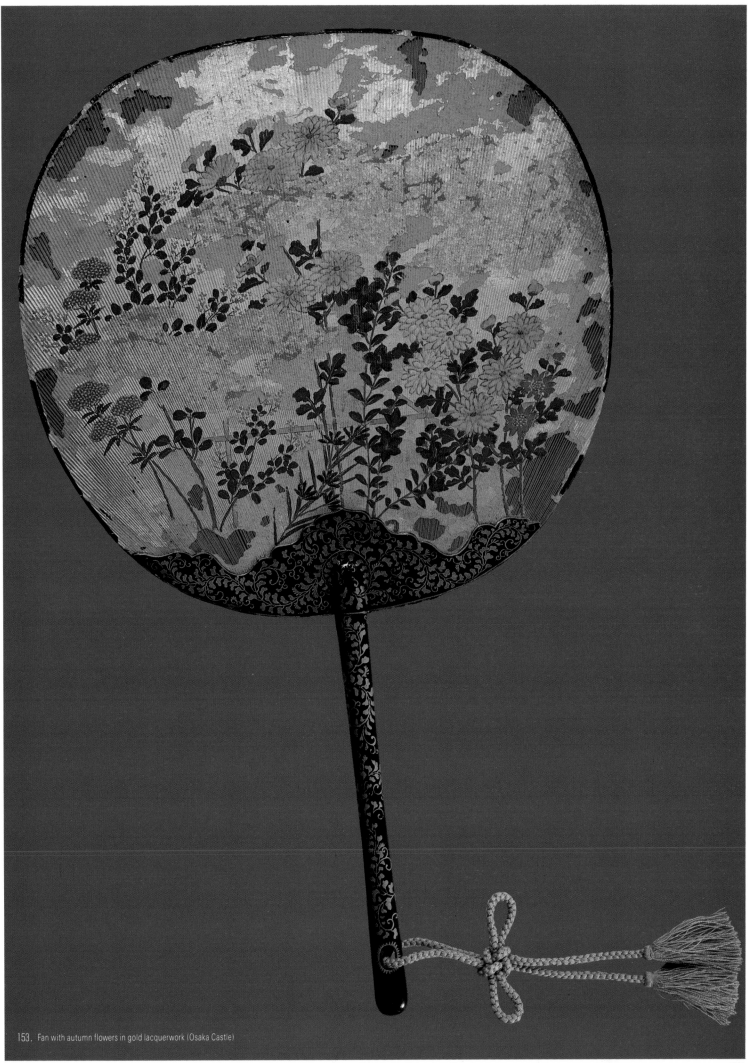

153. Fan with autumn flowers in gold lacquerwork (Osaka Castle)

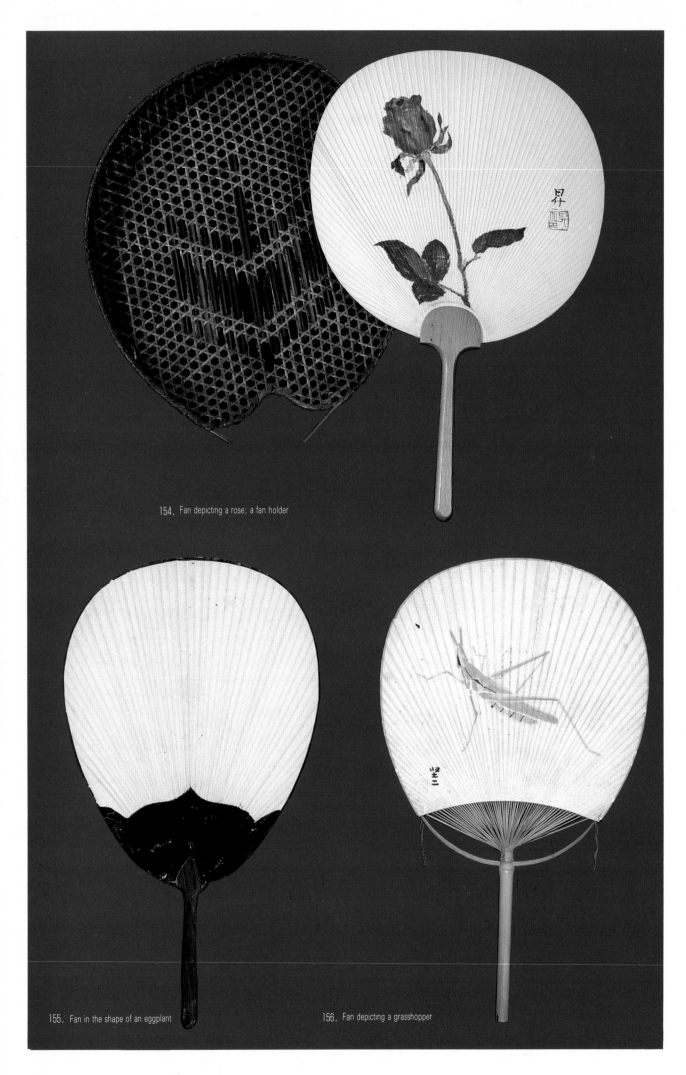

154. Fan depicting a rose; a fan holder

155. Fan in the shape of an eggplant

156. Fan depicting a grasshopper

SMOKING ACCESSORIES

喫煙具

In the latter half of the sixteenth century, tobacco was brought to Japan by the Europeans. As is evident from *uk-iyoe* depicting courtesans smoking long pipes, full cultural fruition includes a high level of smoking accessories.

157. Tobacco tray

158. Tobacco tray with ivy pattern in gold lacquerwork

159. Tobacco tray with snowflake pattern in mother-of-pearl

160. Tobacco tray

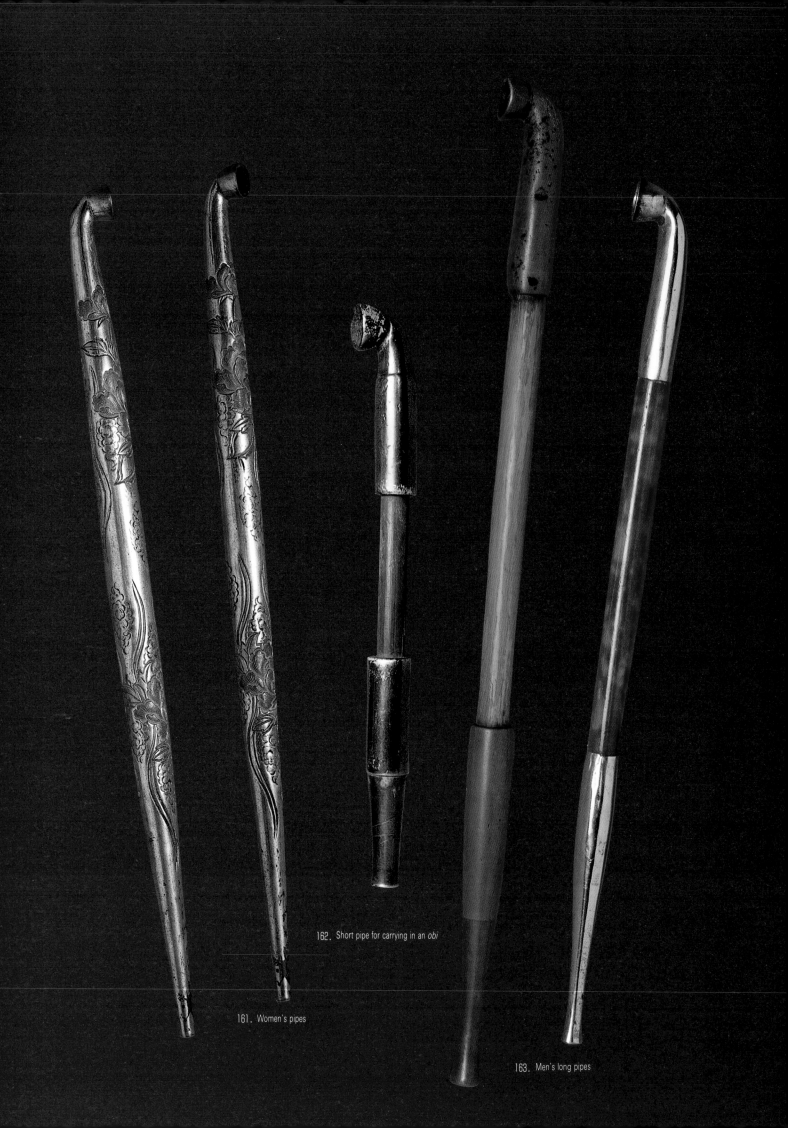

162. Short pipe for carrying in an *obi*

161. Women's pipes

163. Men's long pipes

164. Tobacco pouch

165. Tobacco pouches

166. *Hakoseko* (a pouch)

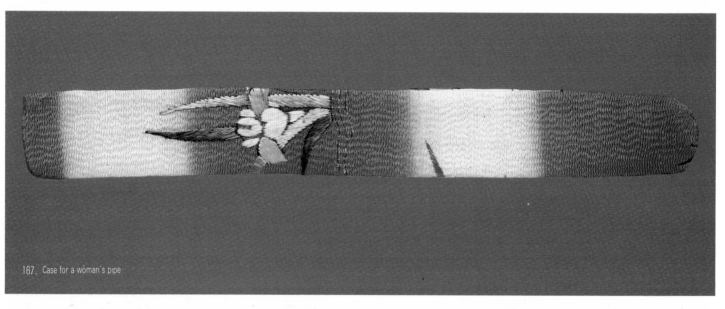

167. Case for a woman's pipe

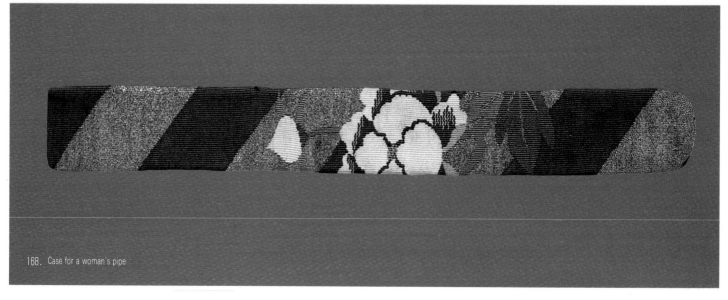

168. Case for a woman's pipe

169. *Inrō* with goldfish in mother-of-pearl

170. *Inrō* with goldfish in gold lacquerware *zonsei*

171. *Inrō* with *hōrin* pattern

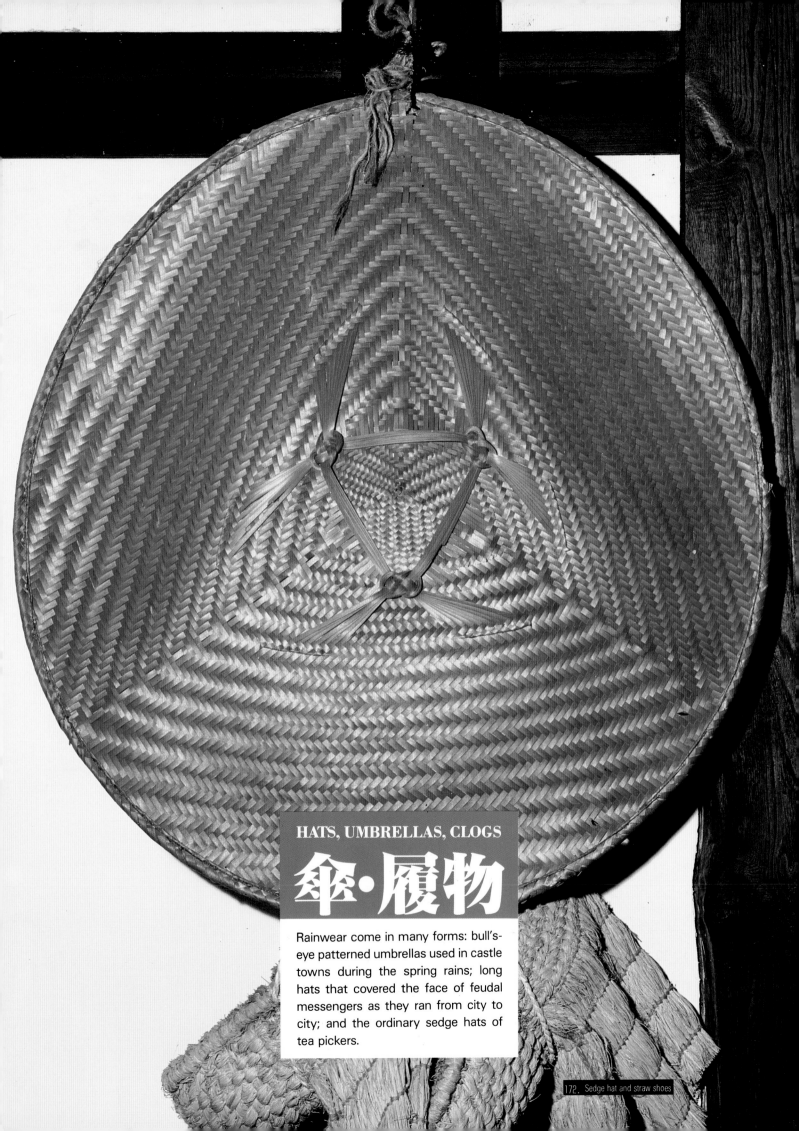

HATS, UMBRELLAS, CLOGS

傘・履物

Rainwear come in many forms: bull's-eye patterned umbrellas used in castle towns during the spring rains; long hats that covered the face of feudal messengers as they ran from city to city; and the ordinary sedge hats of tea pickers.

172. Sedge hat and straw shoes

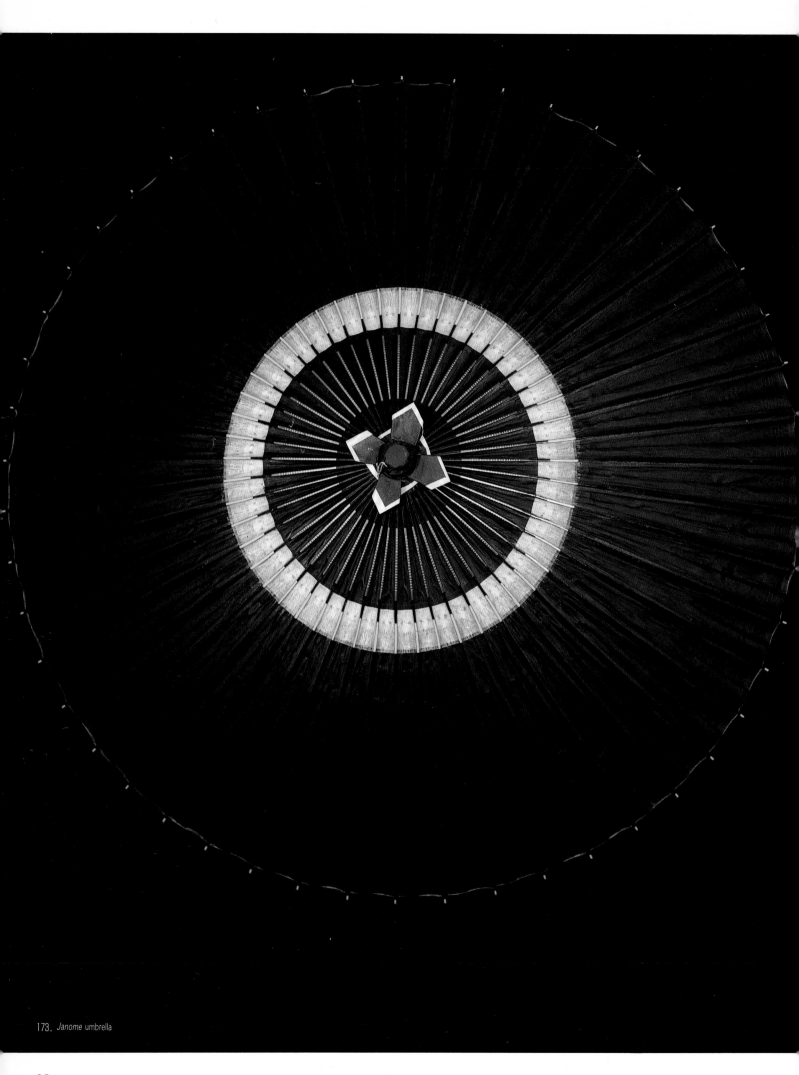

173. *Janome umbrella*

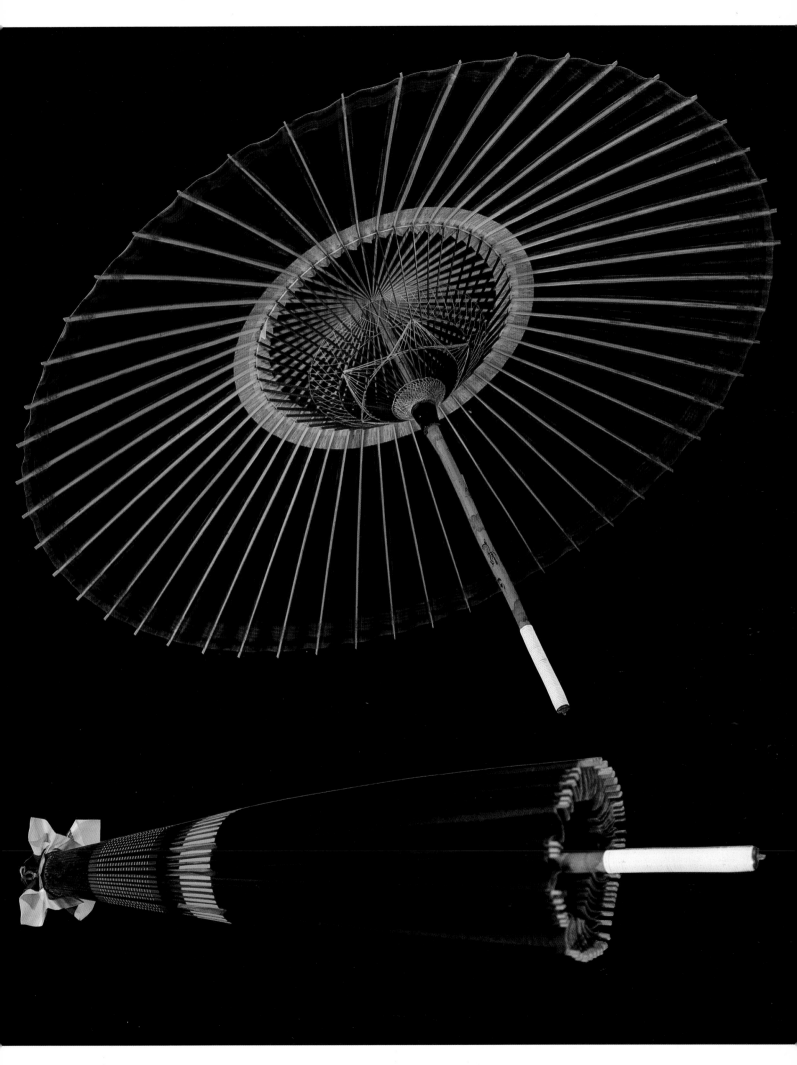

174. Warrior's helmet with family crest

175. Warrior's helmet with family crest

176. Warrior's helmet with family crest

177. Warrior's helmet with family crest

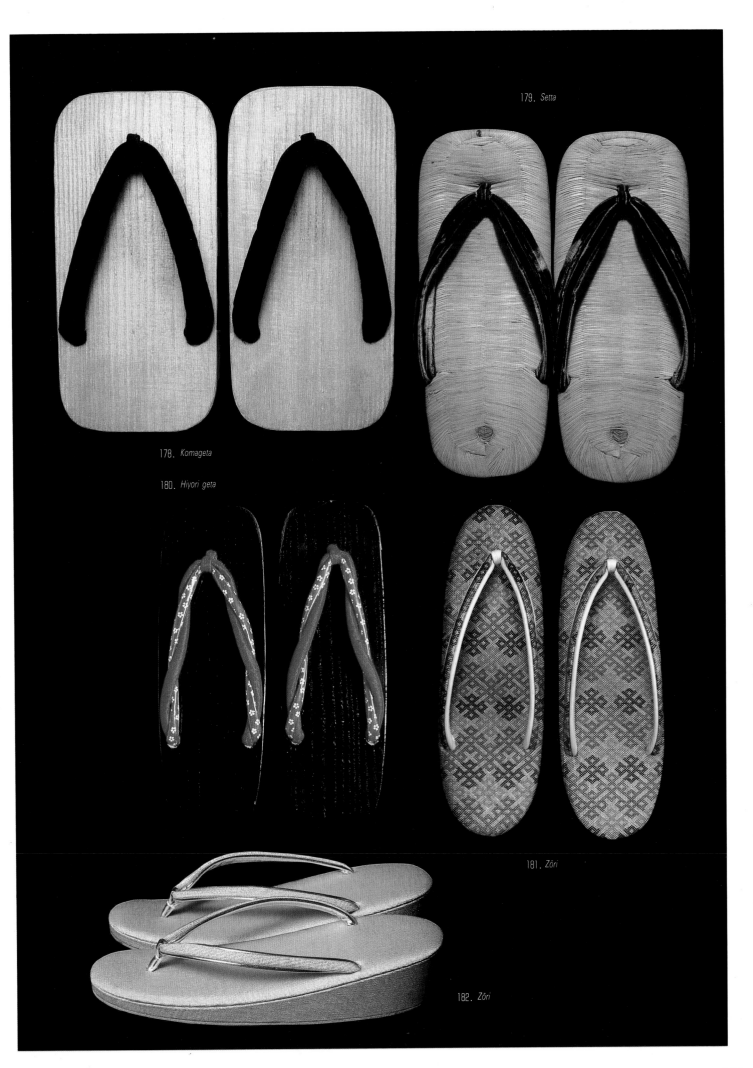

178. *Komageta*

180. *Hiyori geta*

179. *Setta*

181. *Zōri*

182. *Zōri*

YUKATA

浴衣

Composing a poem in midsummer virtually requires the poet to be wearing a *yukata*. Men with their *yukata* tucked up as they mill about during a summer festival are a handsome sight, the indigo of their robes giving a coolness to the hot streets.

183. *Yukata* with swallows-on-willow pattern

184. Pine-bark pattern (*matsukawa-bishi*)

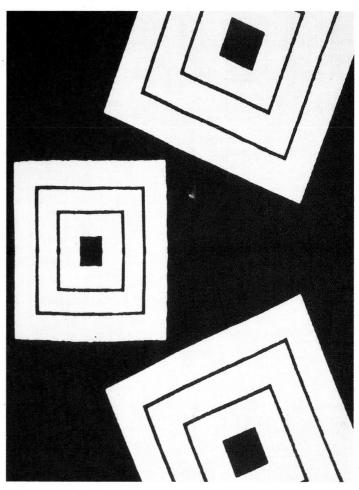

185. *Shibaraku* pattern, used in Kabuki

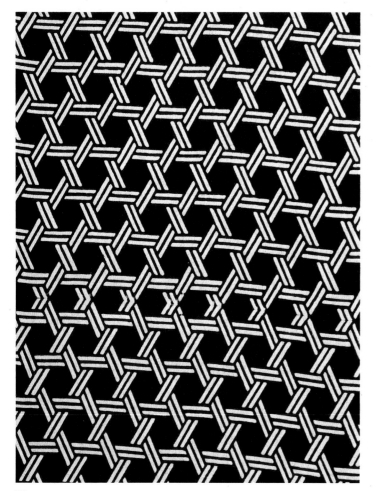

186. Woven pattern (*kagome*)

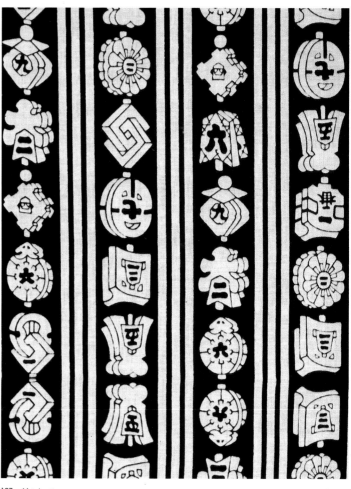

187. *Matoi* pattern

188. Sweet flag pattern (*shōbu*)

189. Bellflower pattern (*kikyō*)

190. Rhonbus pattern (*hishi*)

191. Autumn flowers pattern (*akikusa*)

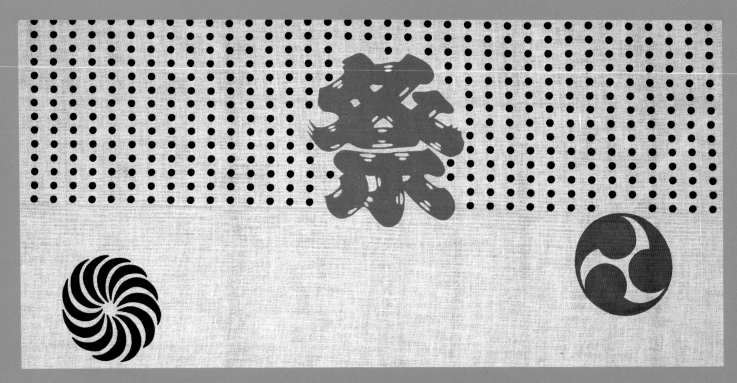

192. Hand towel with the character *matsuri* (festival)

193. Hand towel "blizzard of cherry blossoms" crest

194. Hand towel with crest

195. Hand towel with figure of an anchor

196. Hand towel with geese

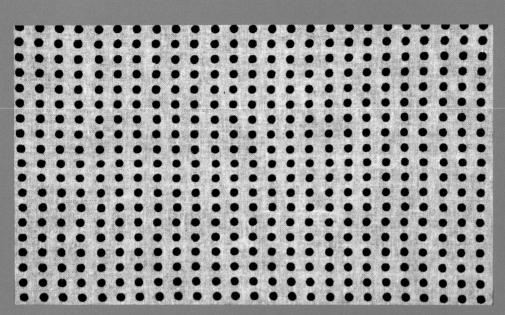

197. Hand towel with a spotted pattern

198. Hand towel depicting a dog

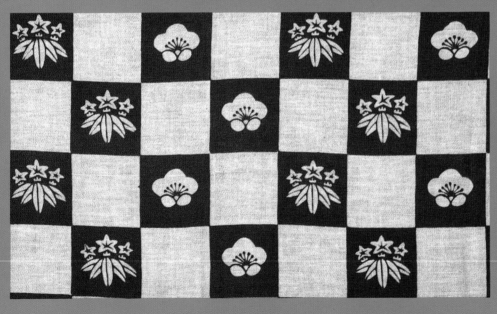

199. Checked hand towel with bamboo and plum blossom figures

HANTEN

半纏

A *hanten* is a short coat, a common use of which was as a sort of advertisement for a business firm. The name and mark of the employer were dyed on the collar and back. The coat, also called a *happi*, is worn today at festivals and bargain sales.

201. *Haori* with "six coins" crest

202. Fireman's leather *hanten*

203. Fireman's leather *hanten* with "flowers in triple tortoiseshell" crest (Nara Prefecture Art Museum)

204. Leather *hanten* (Nara Prefecture Art Museum)

205. Leather *hanten*

206. Fireman's leather *hanten*

207. Woman diver's clothing

208. Chanchanko

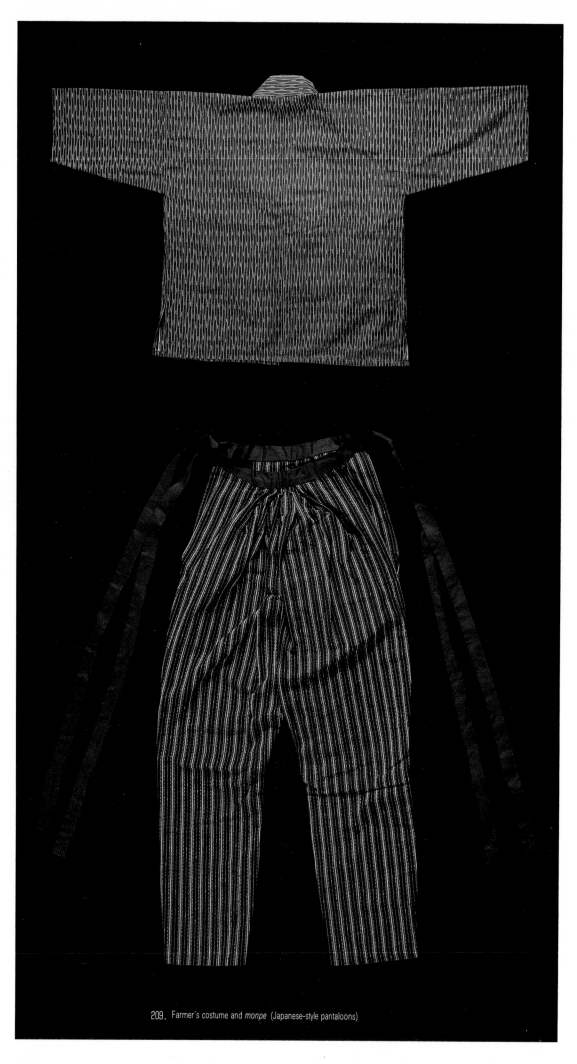

209. Farmer's costume and *monpe* (Japanese-style pantaloons)

TSUTSUGAKI

筒描

Tsutsugaki is a dyeing technique. Yūzen, bingata, and sarasa patterns are representative of this technique. The tsutsugaki and the sashiko, or quilted coat, display the clothing maker's art.

210. Cloth with peacock and flower pattern made by *tsutsugaki* process

211. Cloth with flower and phoenix pattern made by *tsutsugaki* process

212. Cloth with bamboo, plum blossom, and crane pattern made by *tsutsugaki* process

213. Cloth with *noshi* pattern made by *tsutsugaki* process

214. Cloth with *kicchō* (lucky omen) pattern made by *tsutsugaki* process

215. Cloth with phoenix and paulownia pattern made by *tsutsugaki* process

216. Cloth with phoenix and paulownia pattern made by *tsutsugaki* process

217. Cloth with *iwaimusubi* pattern made by *tsutsugaki* process

218. Cloth with wave, sand, and fan pattern made by *tsutsugaki* process

219. Cloth with paulownia-in-circle pattern made by *tsutsugaki* process

220. Cloth with *kotobuki* (longevity character) pattern made by *tsutsugaki* process

221. *Kasuri* with crane, turtle, and *noshi* pattern

222. *Kasuri* with chrysanthemum and arabesque pattern

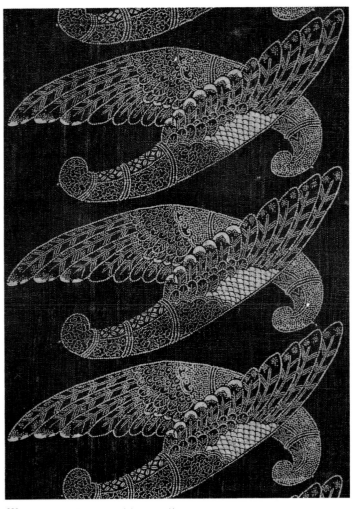

223. Cloth with *habōki* pattern made by *tsutsugaki* process

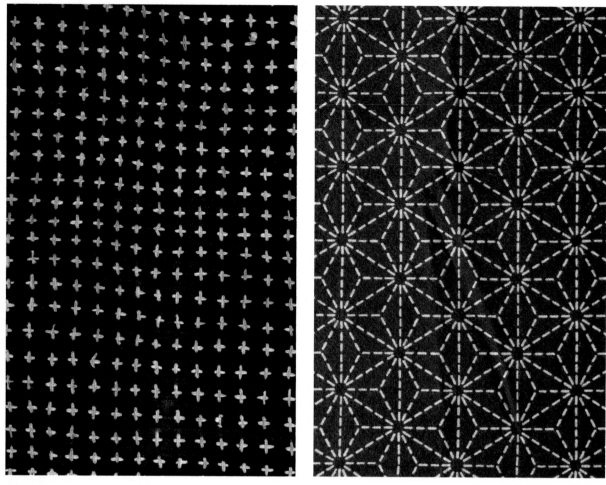

224. *Sashiko* with pattern of crosses

225. *Sashiko* with hemp flower pattern

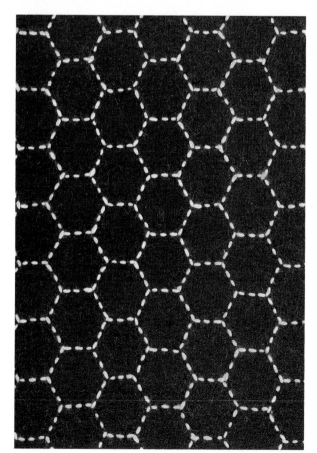

226. *Sashiko* with tortoiseshell pattern

227. *Sashiko* with flowers-in-diamonds pattern

道具

Sewing tools bring to mind scenes of the past: a mother working late into the night by the light of a dim lamp, her sewing box beside her: a young woman spinning thread and weaving cloth as she dreams of the day she will be married.

229. Spinning wheel

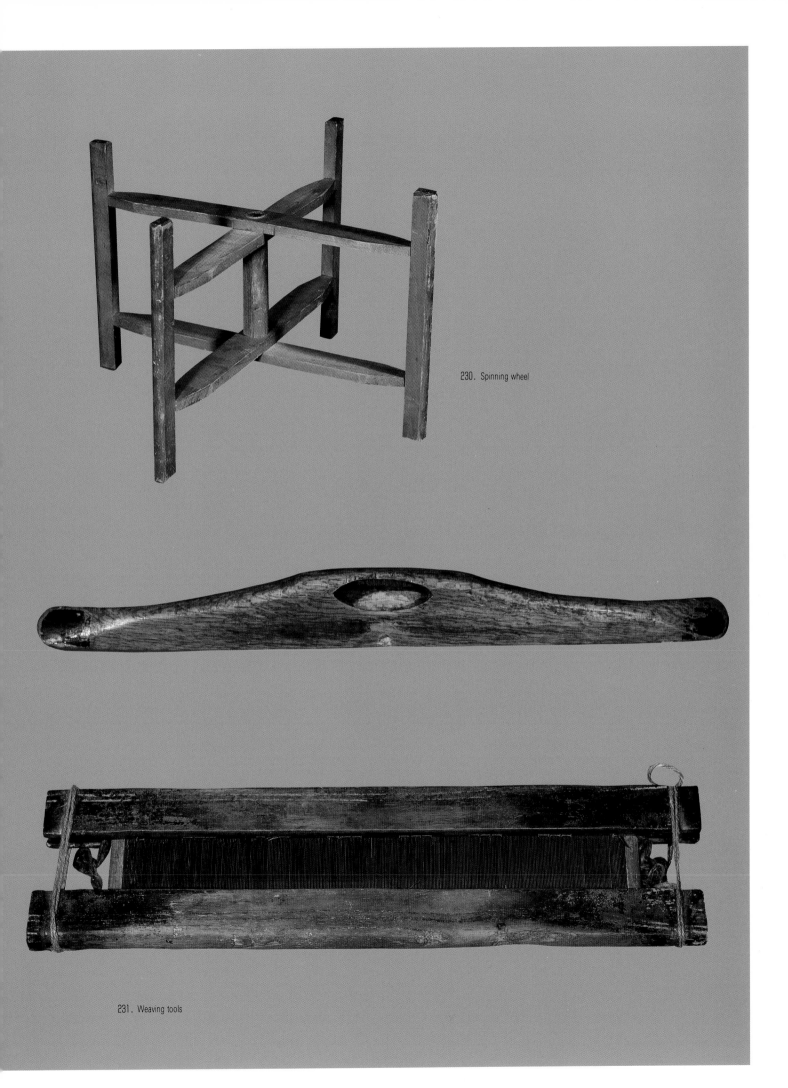

230. Spinning wheel

231. Weaving tools

232. Sewing box

BELIEFS

信仰

Clothes unique to religious functions and purposes appear in various forms: a monk's surplice, a stone *jizo*'s red bib, the white robes of pilgrims as they make their way from temple to temple. In clothing resides people's prayers.

233. Hand towel with the character *matsuri*

234. *Tairyō* ("great catch") *iwaigi*

235. *Tairyō iwaigi*

236. *Gojō-no-kesa* (monk's surplice)

238. *Fuhō* (black monk's robe) and white robe

237. *Chūkei* folding fan

239. Festival *hanten*

240. Festival *hanten* with Toyama plum-blossom crest

based on flowers, animals, and the like. Examples of the former include *seikaiha* (p. 17), *tachiwaki* (p. 19), and *matsukawa-bishi* (p. 24).

sashiko: material made from several layers of cotton cloth sewn tightly together. It was originally used to reinforce other garments, but eventually came to have various designs and be used for coats and the like.
sensu: *see* fan
setta: strong *zōri* made by attaching leather to the bottom of bamboo-sheath *zōri*
shinshibari: a process in which cloth is stretched over fine bamboo poles (*shinshi*) for dyeing, starching, etc.
shōzoku: clothing; a garment or costume
sobatsugi: a sleeveless *haori* worn by samurai; also used in Noh drama
sōshibori: tie-dyeing
Sōtōka: an ornament of artificial flowers, inserted in the hair
sukiya bag (**J. sukiya-bukuro**): a small, colorful handbag

tabako bon: a small open box in which smoking implements are placed
tabi: footwear made of sturdy cloth, fastened with metal clasps, with the big toe separated from the others; worn by workmen and also on certain formal occasions
Tsutsugaki: a dyeing process in which starch is forced out a small hole at the end of a persimmon-juice-stained tube or cone onto a fabric to make a desired pattern. When the fabric is dyed, the starched parts resist the dye, leaving behind the desired pattern. This technique is used for *Yūzen*-dyeing, *hanten*, banners, curtains, *noren*, etc.

yukata: a light robe worn after a bath or in the summer

zonsei: a lacquerware technique perhaps originally used in Ming dynasty China and brought to Japan during the Edo period. A design is either painted on with colored lacquer or carved into the object, after which colored lacquer is filled into the carved parts.
zōri: sandals the surface of which are made of woven straw, rush, bamboo, etc.